BEST OF JAMES MO

Cover photo by Lee Strickland

ISBN 978-1-4234-7782-2

7777 W. BLUEMOUND RD. P.O. BOX 13819 MILWAUKEE, WI 53213

Visit Hal Leonard Online at
www.halleonard.com

JAMES MORRISON BIO 2008

A testimony to the strength of the songs on James Morrison's debut album *Undiscovered* is that it yielded no fewer than five singles – "You Give Me Something," "Wonderful World," "The Pieces Don't Fit Anymore," "Undiscovered" and "One Last Chance." The songs were simple yet beautifully written, each giving James's raw, bluesy voice a platform to work its powerful magic. There was no bull, no clichés, no schmaltz. And a lot of people liked that.

Undiscovered went to No 1 in Britain, Top 25 in America and won him the 2007 Brit Award for Best Male (he was also nominated for Best Single and Best Newcomer). James's debut sold over two million copies world-wide and he became the biggest selling British male solo artist of 2006. He was just 21 – but had already accumulated enough life experience to give his candid folk-soul songs genuine emotional content. By many people's standards he'd had a tough, itinerant childhood, a broken family and endless house moves – although he'd be the first to shrug and say it was no big deal. But he'd also admit that most of the emotion in his singing has come from his upbringing.

James's reputation as a must-see live performer soared. Following his jaw dropping, first ever TV performance on *Later With Jools Holland* he went on to play amazing shows to adoring crowds: including the V festival twice in one day – in 2006 so many people came to see him in one of the smaller tents that he was invited to give an impromptu performance on the main stage; last year he played a full set on the main stage. Then there was the Royal Variety Performance, the Concert for Diana and the more traditional 3 sold-out UK tours. He did the Peace One Day concert at the Royal Albert Hall – and had one of those moments where he suddenly realized that his life had changed forever. "Just before I went on I was watching Yusuf Islam and I thought, I'm on after Cat Stevens! I remember being at home with my dad listening to his albums during the darkest times, the best of times…" James has subsequently provided vocals on Yusuf's new album.

He toured Europe, Australia and Japan, did three separate tours of America, gigging coast to coast. He also supported John Mayer on his large outdoor tour of the US. He gave an acoustic rendition of "You Give Me Something" on national TV on NBC's *Today* as well as Jimmy Kimmel's show, and performed on Jay Leno's show twice at the host's invitation. James loved the musical appreciation in the American South in particular. "People were awesome in Alabama – really friendly, loud and lairy. Even if you play a quiet song, afterwards they just go YEAH!!!"

It was an amazing time. But sometimes, when he wasn't onstage, or with the band, he'd feel an acute sense of being increasingly cut off from the people who mattered: his friends and family back in Cornwall – where his mother had finally settled with James, his brother Laurie and sister Hayley when James was 11, and where James had refined his self-taught singing and guitar-playing by busking in Newquay. Most importantly of all, he missed his long-term girlfriend Gill, who had inspired "You Give Me Something" and, during a rocky patch in their relationship, "The Pieces Don't Fit Anymore."

The further James Morrison travelled, both physically and career-wise, the more he craved the people he loved. "Everything I'd felt close to just disappeared," he says. "You do lose your mind a bit; you haven't got any routines. And sometimes all I'd think about on the road would be Gill – but we'd lose contact. So when I got home it'd feel like we were starting again."

He finally stopped in August 2007. For two weeks. And then he sat down to write and record the notoriously difficult **Second Album**. And at first it did prove difficult. He tried to write rockier, harder tunes – as glimpsed on *Undiscovered*'s "Call the Police," which touched on the subject of domestic violence. "I went for something with a bit more electric guitar but in the end it just sounded contrived."

The pressure was on and it was making him try too hard, too self-consciously. "As soon as I'd get something good I'd think about it and screw it up." And then the penny dropped: "Just go for what you're feeling at the time. That's how I worked on the first album, and in a way I think that's some of the reason why people liked it. It wasn't trying too hard."

And so the people who really made him feel, the ones who became the subjects of his songs on *Undiscovered* – his family and friends – his relationship with each of them, and the new chapters in all their lives, became central to the new album. James went with whatever and whoever was on his mind, and took it from there. The songs began to flow.

"I've called the album *Songs for You, Truths for Me* because that's what I feel it is. It's songs for Gill and everyone else. But for me they're truths. They're how I feel. I've got a song called 'Love is Hard.' In fact, there are three songs with 'love' in the title – and I never thought I'd do that, but that's the way it went. 'Love is Hard' is about when you're deep in it and it hurts a lot of the time. You're fighting, or not always agreeing, you might be away from each other and you've still got to be strong. So the album's a collection of truths I'd learnt in the previous year. It just turned out that way: I knew I didn't want to write about being on the road. I can only write about what I feel."

In the end, James enlisted many of the same collaborators from *Undiscovered* to work with him on *Songs for You, Truths for Me.* He also added a new fan, One Republic's Ryan Tedder, to that list. The Nashville string quartet also feature once again. "I know we work well together now – it'll take a lot for me to work with someone new."

There is also a notable collaboration on this record, one of the only things his debut album didn't have, a fantastic duet with Nelly Furtado on the epic "Broken Strings."

Songs for You, Truths for Me is a classic James Morrison record that once again showcases his distinctive, raw, soulful style – but takes it to the next level. "It's less playful, more to the point," he says. "But I haven't consciously gone for a different sound. With me, it always comes down to the lyric, the melody, and the rest flows from that. But I've definitely tapped into my feelings about life more on this album, rather than writing about characters on the bus ("Wonderful World"), or whatever. I was just letting stuff flow through me."

James Morrison's big, unashamedly romantic heart and generous spirit shines through like a beacon. *Songs for You, Truths for Me* sees the wide eyed soul-boy become a wiser man. With this he shines once more on a brilliant new collection of songs and cathartic truths.

BROKEN STRINGS

Words and Music by JAMES MORRISON,
NINA WOODFORD and FRASIER SMITH

Moderately

Let me hold ___ you for the last ___ time. It's the last _

_ chance to feel a - gain. ___ But you broke ___ me, ___ now I can't _

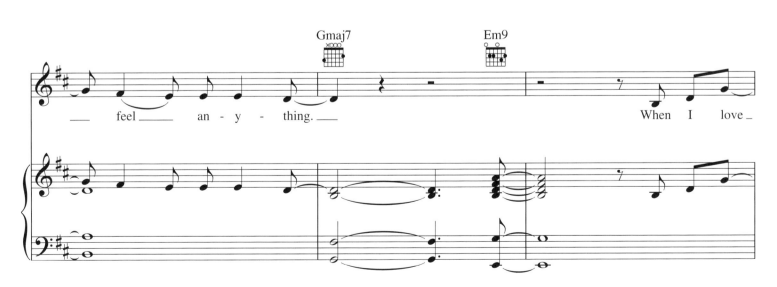

_ feel ___ an - y - thing. ___ When I love _

BETTER MAN

Words and Music by JAMES MORRISON,
JULIAN GALLAGHER and KIM RICHEY

NOTHING EVER HURT LIKE YOU

Words and Music by JAMES MORRISON,
PAUL BARRY and MARK TAYLOR

ONCE, WHEN I WAS LITTLE

Words and Music by JAMES MORRISON,
MARTIN TEREFE and DAN WILSON

Moderately slow

I was the one who would al - ways jump in first. ___
We could build a rock - et, fly to the moon. ___

I did - n't think twice to look ___ be - hind. ___
Leave Tues - day morn - ing ___ and ___ be

back 'fore noon.
Got such a good feel - ing, just from
And there was - n't noth - in', just noth - in'

THE PIECES DON'T FIT ANYMORE

Words and Music by JAMES MORRISON,
STEVE ROBSON and MARTIN BRAMMER

Moderately slow

Mm, mm, _____ mm, mm. _____

I've been twist-ing and turn-ing in a space that's too
You pulled me un - der so I had to give

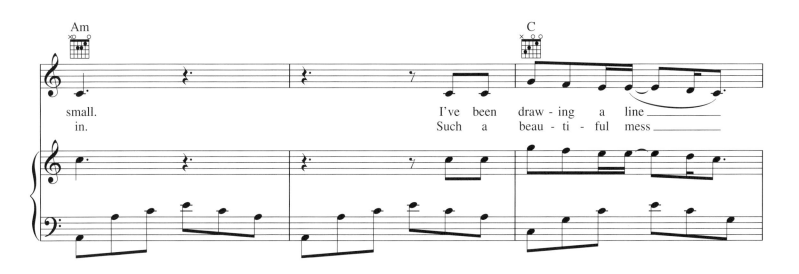

small. I've been draw-ing a line _____
in. Such a beau-ti-ful mess _____

PLEASE DON'T STOP THE RAIN

Words and Music by JAMES MORRISON
and RYAN TEDDER

PRECIOUS LOVE

Words and Music by JAMES MORRISON
and JOHN SHANKS

THIS BOY

Words and Music by JAMES MORRISON
and TIM KELLETT

UNDER THE INFLUENCE

Words and Music by JAMES MORRISON,
STEVE McEWAN and JAMES HOGARTH

Once you've had a taste _ of it, there's no go-ing back. _ Once you've had a taste _ of it, there's

no go - ing back. _

no go - ing back. _

D.S. al Coda
(take 2nd ending)

CODA

What-

Drums

UNDISCOVERED

Words and Music by JAMES MORRISON,
STEVE ROBSON and MARTIN BRAMMER

WONDERFUL WORLD

Words and Music by JAMES MORRISON
and FRANCIS WHITE

I've been down so low peo-ple look at me and they
Some-times I feel so full of love it just comes spill-ing

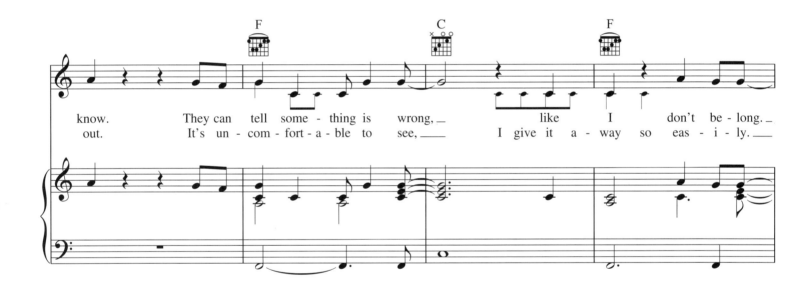

know. They can tell some-thing is wrong, ___ like I don't be-long.
out. It's un-com-fort-a-ble to see, ___ I give it a-way so eas-i-ly. ___

___ Well, star-ing through a win-dow, stand-ing out-
___ But if I had some-one, I would do

Recorded a half step lower.

68

YOU MAKE IT REAL

Words and Music by JAMES MORRISON
and PAUL BARRY

here with me, I know which way to turn. You al - ways give me

some - where, some - where I can run.

D.S. al Coda

CODA

you make it real for me.

You make it real for me.

YOU GIVE ME SOMETHING

Words and Music by JAMES MORRISON
and FRANCIS WHITE

You on-ly stay __ with me __ in the morn __ ing. _____
You on-ly wait-ed up __ for __ hours _____

You on-ly hold __ me when __ I sleep. ___
just to spend a lit-tle time a-lone with me. ___

I was meant __ to tread __ the wa — ter, _____
And I can say I've nev — er brought __ you flow — ers. _____